Keep the

Dance

Pat Grieco

Keep the Dance

Other Books by Pat Grieco

The Art of Nauga Farming

Compulsion

Rhetoric

The Book of Light

Grieco

Copyright 2019 by Pat Grieco

All rights reserved
First Print Edition

Print edition produced in the United States of America

Cover art: Pat Grieco

All characters appearing in this work are fictitious. Any resemblance to real persons, living or dead, is purely coincidental.

Print ISBN: 978-1-7324688-2-5

Pen and Lute
www.penandlute.com

The final approval for this literary material is granted by the author.

Library of Congress Control Number: 2019907311

Distributed Publication
Lexington, KY
Middletown, DE
San Bernardino. CA

Keep the Dance

DEDICATION

For every heart that yearns to sing

Keep the

Dance

Pat Grieco

Keep the Dance

Grieco

Sometimes, I need her to be strong.
Sometimes, I need her to be weak.
And sometimes, I just need her.

Contents

Come	1
A Table Set for One	2
Two Stones	4
A Glance	6
Beauty	8
His first and only love	10
Day begins anew	12
Be Simple in Love	15
Chance	17
Be Thou But A Dream	19
Until I met you	22
Only one thing	24
Late for Dinner	27
Believe	29
Shall I compare thee	31
One Sure Measure	37
Imzadi	38
A wondrous thing	41
Before I Knew	43
I Do Not Love You	44
Keep the Dance	47
Be With Me Love	48
Let's married be	49
Renewal	51

Wedding Advice 52
Always 54
A Woman's Plea 56
Memory of your kiss 60
A rose to remember you by 62
At First Sight Too 64
Oblivious 65
His Safe Return 67
All the difference 69
Regardless 74
What is known 76
With a kiss 77
On the end of things 80
If I should forget you 86

Come

Come to me my Love
and build a bed of flowers
in the meadow
where we will lie
and share the secrets of our hearts
beneath the warming sun.

Sheltered in my arms
you will know no loss of self
but share in all I am
and may yet be
while I will gain your strength
and faith in the way of things.

Together we will have no doubts
but face the day with joyful hope
that it shall be ever so
while two hearts keep one dream
within this place and moment
where all things may yet be
if you will but come to me.

Grieco

A Table Set for One

A table set for one
is a lonely thing.

One glass,
to wash away the hidden fears.

One fork,
to feed the ego.

A spoon,
to feed ourselves our cup of truth.

One knife,
to cut to the heart of things.

There is no shame
to dine alone.
But each glance,
each bite,
reminds us of our setting.

Music heard by one
lacks the subtle binding
of its mischief.

The message meant for two
is lost upon the soul
that dines alone.

The food is rich.
The company is cordial,
and the drinks are on the house.
But laughter does not chase
the clever turn of phrase

Keep the Dance

and nowhere can the heart find rest
but on an empty sleeve.

A table set for one
is a lonely thing.

Grieco

Two Stones

There you are
standing
in that first moment of meeting.

In that moment
there is an instant recognition,
that sense
of stone meeting stone
in that seamless way
that reveals a foundation
built upon before
though long abandoned
and forgot.

Memories fade,
lives pass,
and time erases much
between the then and now
'til only echoes sound
and traces remain
of what was before.

Yet what is forgotten
still remains
and may be built upon anew
with stone meeting stone
in common cause
'til semblance of the past
be found again
if fate be kind
and time allow rebuilding
of what was lost.

Keep the Dance

And if past is future
yet to be,
where stone meets stone
is the meeting place
between the two
that builds the now.

There you are
and all else fades
'til only two remain
as time slows,
stone meets stone,
and all things become possible.

Grieco

A Glance

I loved her,
and still do
if truth be told,
since first we passed.

It was just a glance
that caught me so
and being snared
found myself enmeshed
in feeling
long thought absent
from the world.

For some
a glance
is but a passing gaze,
forgotten in an instant,
of no more importance
than a second's thought,
a moment's distraction
from the task ahead.

But for me
it shows the soul
in all its depths
and twists
and flaws
and revealed her so to me.

No secrets there,
no hidden place
within that kind and gentle face.
It was marked
by joy and sorrow both

Keep the Dance

with hopes and dreams
held dear
and not forgot
though put aside
as is the way of things.

It held such strength
that made me stop
and give my interest,
give my gaze,
and more.

Ah chance,
that granted such a glance
and found such a soul,
unfixed and free,
in joy and beauty both unbound
with heart held close
'til one be found
to share its journey.

All this I saw in moment's gaze
as eyes caught mine
and passed
to wander onward
to more weighty stuff.

All this,
and I am certain
that I shall never love another
as I loved her then,
from this,
a single
glance.

Grieco

Beauty

You ask me if I find you beautiful.
I cannot answer
for I do not know what beauty is.

I only know
you make my heart sing
and my spirit soar
among the clouds of heaven.

I hear your voice
and lose all sense
of anything
beyond the here and now.

Entranced,
I can but hope
to catch a glimpse
of your perfect face.

I do not know what beauty is
but I know a happiness
that fills my waking hours
and replaces hope
for now I have all
I hoped for.

You are the essence of my dreams
but in this,
my sleepless state,
I live a truth,
in form and substance,
which makes my nighttime dreams
but shadows of this present fact.

Keep the Dance

Do not ask again.
I can but answer with words
that do not convey
the meaning of my heart,
the vision of these eyes,
or the spirit
that yearns to be with you.

You ask
and I can only answer
with every moment of my life
spent in rapt devotion
and in love
that knows no boundaries
or limitations.

You are the meaning of my life,
and if life is beautiful
then it is certain
that I find you so.

Grieco

His first and only love

Happy the man who lives on the sea
with her constant embrace
soothing him,
holding him to her.

There can be no other mistress,
no true wife ashore,
for she has him captured
from the moment of their meeting,
from that first salty kiss,
that first sweet enticement
and sweet caress
as waves and wind
become the sum of things.

He is lost to all else.
Nothing else will claim him.
No one else will have his heart
as she does.

He is at peace upon her bosom,
at rest, eased by her presence,
her sure and constant touch,
the vastness of her spirit,
and her endless reach.

He may move upon her
and she will change beneath him,
always the same, always different,
inviting and forbidding,
both warm and cold the same.

He cares not for her moods,
and avoids them when he can,

Keep the Dance

but as a true and faithful lover
endures the sudden tempests,
survives the mounting storms
to return when she is calm
and countenance is fair
and welcoming once more.

Still, he will return when he should not,
when wrath is still a moment's chance
and sea a cold and heartless place
of fury and despair.
For she is his first and only love
and he would suffer much
to be with her again.

And at the end,
when she endures and he cannot,
he will sleep,
content within her bounty,
the very soul of his belovéd,
and dream an endless dream
of happiness
and her.

Grieco

Day begins anew

Sad and lonely face
upon a plain but well-set frame,
the years heavy with the emptiness
that spoke from every line and crease
that marked her as alone,
heavy with the knowledge
of her fate.

She shopped for what she needed,
the food within the cart
simple fare,
bread,
milk,
essentials all,
complete for one,
lacking only one more
to make a truly satisfying meal.

In her smile still lay hope,
but her stance
spoke of empty days and nights
unfilled with laughter
or with love.

Set apart by chance or fate
the end was still the same,
a driveway with but one car
and silence
waiting past the gate.

Inside, a table waits
for a simple setting,
a wine filled glass
and dinner on a single plate,

Keep the Dance

unadorned except for flower,
palest red,
in slender vase
reflecting sunset's last full rays
before the coming night.

Against the darkness
she will light a single candle,
and by that meager flickering flame
eat
until she has her fill
of simple fare,
of silence there unshared,
and night's slow measured tread.

When done,
she will clear the table,
wash that plate and glass,
and with deliberate pace
ready self and place
for the day to come.

Finished,
she will retreat to bed
in sheltered room
and the comfort
of a worn and faded spread
upon sheets of white.

Closing eyes,
she shall remember less
and, with slowing breath,
dream of two plates
and wine filled glasses
ready for the couple
who in shared delight
rejoice in company

Grieco

treasured and beloved.

**Sleeping,
she will banish loneliness
until sun steals her
from her slumber,
from her dreams,
and day begins anew.**

Keep the Dance

Be Simple in Love

Be simple in Love.
Release expectations.
Give unreservedly.
Ask for nothing.
Share dreams.
Be innocent.
Be kind.

Be simple in Love.
Be two but always one.
Be separate but never apart.
Listen to what is meant.
Laugh, but never at.
Do not confuse want with need.
Know when not to ask.
Tell when it merits telling.

Be simple in Love.
Wake in wonder at the beauty of it.
See the world through newborn eyes.
Walk as though the path was new
and fresh to the errant wanderer.

Be.
Hold each moment
'til the next should come.
Live the dream
to make it real and whole
'til all else fades
and there be only this.

Sleep,
but only as you must,
and wake to simple things;

Grieco

a smile,
a kiss,
a touch,
the warmth of sheets
against the morning chill.

Enjoy the present sharing of it
and look not past
to what the day may bring.

Be simple in Love.

Keep the Dance

Chance

She'd never met him
but she'd known him forever.
They talked with the ease of old lovers,
words and thoughts fitting effortlessly
together
as though their minds and hearts
had spent the time needed
for their souls to mesh,
to join in easy union.

But they had met too soon
or too late.
He was perhaps too old
and she just young enough
to have no doubts
but old enough
to regret the loss
as he stood to go.

She saw him later
sitting with the one he came with
and stopped to briefly chat
of this and that
resting her hand gently
once,
twice,
in a wistful gesture of possessiveness
and wishful thoughts.

She promised she'd be in touch
but she lied,
the sort of lie one makes
when desire is balanced
by present needs

Grieco

and reality.

He was taken.
She was not
and so they came from different worlds.
Fated to be together
they were kept apart
by different ties of experience,
of companionship,
and of time.

They'd met as destined
on that warm October day
with joy a heartbeat
and one decision away
but she doubted her place in this.
She yearned for more
but dreaded less
yet lingered with unsure emotion
fingering the business card he gave her
promising herself she'd contact him,
if not today
then soon,
soon,
to see what future lay in wait
and chance allowed.

No.
Perhaps she'd wait
and come here yet again
to see if fate would bring him to her.
And if it did,
then,
then she'd know
that this was meant to be
and she could trust herself to chance
and to him.

Be Thou But A Dream

Do not go,
but let me stand
within your light.
Is it night?
I know not
for you do dazzle me.

Though darkness shrouds
the living land,
I stand reflected
in your eyes
an empty husk,
'til by your gaze
I am filled.

Oh gentle night,
embrace me
with your shadowed arms
and hold me
to your darkened breast
or I shall burst
with light
and bring forth day.

Behold,
a star does shine
within this darkest night
to bring forth happiness
where once
was but desolation.

I know not
what I was
ere glance from you

Grieco

transformed this shell,
this fragile clay,
from ignorance
to blazing bliss.

I am not now
the man you see,
for 'neath this frame
of bone and flesh
does live a man
renewed.

In hope,
and passioned love
does he reside,
with every thought
consumed by love,
and burning,
purified
to brightest joy.

Stay.
Linger here
within my sight
that I may capture
in my mind
this vision,
this dream.

Let me not wake
but wait,
enchanted,
trapped
within this span of bliss,
this realm of joy.

Keep the Dance

Be thou but a dream
and touch me not
and I shall cry
despairing
of the truth of dreams.

Be thou but a dream
and speak not
and I shall deaf
believe the world
absent of your music.

Be thou but a dream
and love me not
and I shall think
the world a vain
and empty place
and full of sorrow.

Be thou but a dream
and I shall sleep
'til your love
does wake my heart
from slumber.

Be thou but a dream
then let me sleep
and sleeping
know contentment.

Grieco

Until I met you

I knew not the meaning of love
until I met you.

I was alone
but did not know it.

I was waiting for the hand
waiting to hold mine
and make me more
than I am by myself,
searching for the heart
willing to accept mine
in promise and hope,
looking for the mind
to share my dreams
for today and tomorrow.

With you I am complete.
There are no doubts,
no misgivings.
You are the missing part of me,
the part that makes me whole.

Two hearts,
One love.

Two minds,
One thought.

Two lives,
One future
with hearts
and minds
and lives

Keep the Dance

combined
to form the perfect union
now and forever.

I knew not the meaning of love
until I met you.

Grieco

Only one thing

Waste no time with me
for I will waste none with you.
Make each moment together
ours alone.
Save no time for regrets.
Make no time for worry.
Be here,
for I am.

Pay no regard to other things.
Let the world do as it may.
Be happy,
as just we two
share this,
our time together.

Have no expectations.
Only ask for heart,
and mind,
and spirit
to be freely given
without thought of tomorrow,
without fear of today.

Ask for nothing
but receive all in its time.
And if love should follow
measure it not
by the length of days
or span of time
but by the depth of joy
and contentment
felt within.

Keep the Dance

Do not concern yourself
with lesser things,
for they mean nothing
if at the end
your time is counted
in empty moments
held apart from life,
from friends,
from loves,
wasted time
spent on living
without having lived.

Be here
until you are not.
Revel in each moment
until it is past
and then embrace the next
in open joy and gladness.

And if sorrow comes
know it as companion
to the sweeter things.
Each shall pass
leaving only memories
of bright burnt moments
stolen,
but forever owned.

Live the moment.
Seize the chance.
And if we be but friends,
I have too few of those.

And if we become more,
then time will write its tale
upon our hearts

Grieco

whether we will it or not.

And if we be neither
then let us part
with conscious knowledge
of what might yet be.

But,
regardless of the future,
I ask only one thing.
Waste no time with me
for I shall waste none with you.

Keep the Dance

Late for Dinner

"You're late." she said,
turning from the window
as he came through the door.

"I know." he replied,
taking off his coat
and preparing to stay.

"All my life I have stood
and looked through this glass,
watching
and waiting.
Where were you
all this time?"

"Down the street
at the sidewalk café
drinking tea
and waiting for you."

"I never go there."

"I know that now
but I thought you would come
so I stayed."

"How did you find me?"

Moving towards her,
he answered.
"I had wearied of the wait
so I paid my bill
and left to walk a bit
before going home.

Grieco

Then you crossed the street,
looking neither left nor right
but straight ahead,
coming from the market.
I knew it was you,
so I followed."

"Well, you are late
and dinner's almost done."

"I know." he said
and sat at a table
set with remnants of a feast.
"But I would like to share the rest
if you will let me."

Closing the door,
she turned
and moved to seat herself.
"I would welcome the company.
But you are late."

"You did not come."

She gazed upon his face,
searching for the truth
hidden there
and said at last,
"Well we are both here now."

"Yes."

And finding comfort in those words,
they smiled and began to eat.

Believe

Believe.

Believe that I love you
for I do.

Believe that I want you
for I have
since the first instant of our meeting.

Believe that I feel you
every minute of every day
for you are a part of me
beyond description,
beyond understanding,
beyond comprehension.

Believe in the future,
that tomorrow will be better than today,
that dreams are as important
as practical reality,
that hope is but a vision
of better times yet to be.

Believe that things happen for a reason,
that choices may bring us closer
rather than farther apart,
that friendship is companion to love
and that one does not preclude the other.

Believe that you are a constant
in my thoughts
and in my heart.

Grieco

Believe that all things are possible
and they will be.

Believe that distance is unimportant,
that two souls may know their mates,
that two separated by circumstance
may still be one
in heart,
in mind,
in love,
in joy,
if only
we believe.

Keep the Dance

Shall I compare thee

Silly I know
to compare a woman
to a rose.
A rose has thorns
to prick and poke
those who incautiously approach.
A woman…
well perhaps that is a bad example.

A woman in the throes of passion,
eyes screwed shut,
chest heaving,
crying out in joy,
well…
a rose simply isn't that.

It is a thing of beauty,
with fragrance sweet as summer wine
and petals soft as angel's breath
but it does not excite the blood.
It does not caress the mind
with memories of a morning walk
that lingered through the afternoon
to become…
much more.

But still I have it here,
this rose,
pressed thin between the pages
of this long unopened book,
and I am at a loss
as memories surge
at sight of blossom so maintained.

Grieco

Perhaps it is because she wore one
thrust into her hair
that brushed my cheek as we danced
and led my hands to wander
into the depths of tresses
rich and dark
and wonderful to feel,
like silk against my fingertips
and wings of heaven 'gainst my face
when finally, we were alone
and nature's course
most wonderfully took place.

Perhaps it held her scent
and still does
if I but breathe deeply enough
to capture it within
and find myself
again with her.

It has not been long.
An hour,
a day,
a thousand years,
it is all the same
for I have missed her
since she left
and hungered for her presence
each moment she was gone
though I knew it not
until I saw this rose,
waiting,
forgotten 'tween these pages
'til now.

Gently did I pluck it then
and kept it 'gainst the day

Keep the Dance

when memories of such times
must be my comfort
and my curse.

This is not that rose.
It cannot be,
for it is dust
now centuries past
and gone
as are the frames
that bore us then.

But this one,
fragile,
dry,
and faded,
does somehow
bring her here to me
and sparks such ancient love
to vibrant life
that I do hope to see her thus
arrayed against my chest
with rose still tangled
in her unbound hair.

But she is the stuff of dreams
warm to heart and mind
but cold in time and place
as lifetimes pass
and knowing is forgotten.

For I had forgotten,
or so I thought,
her eyes,
her touch,
her scent,
her kiss,

Grieco

but it seems
I have not
though I was content
to believe it so.

Dreams pass.
Hopes fade,
but roses still remain
my memory to sustain,
regardless of the time,
regardless of the frame.
I have traveled long without you
and I would have,
in fact,
what dreams alone impart.

But though I ache to hold you
I cannot.
And though my blood burns bright
with urgent need for you
it is not likely
I will find you here,
in this time,
in this place,
with this most unfortunate blessing
pressed between these pages.

Instead,
it seems I have this rose,
nothing like the woman,
nothing more than touchstone
for memories long laid to rest,
hopes long vanished,
and dreams that touch me
even now
beyond their time.

Keep the Dance

What fool to linger so
when present needs
should move me more
than hopes and dreams
from another time.
But this rose,
this rose does bind me
with such welcomed chains
of memory.

Silly I know
to compare a woman to a rose.
Woman and rose,
skin and petal soft,
hair and flower scent so sweet,
kiss and nectar so intertwined
in deepest dreams within my mind
that rose should bring her
here to me.
And yet,
and yet,
I would have it no other way
except perhaps
to be with her
again.

To feel her full formed flesh
against my skin,
and feel the thunder of emotion
as two raging seas
erased the land between
and by meeting in such urgency
brought forth peace
and such joy
as to shatter all conception of the word.

Grieco

I have no time
to sit and remember so
for I should go
and make much of deeds
that wait for me to do them.

But I would linger
and wonder at what chance
did bring me to this rose.

Silly…

One Sure Measure

Before I learned to speak
your name was on my lips.

Before I breathed
and the fragrant air
filled my lungs
with blissful
knowledge
of your scent,
your image was
engraved in my heart.

Before I knew
what life was
you were my life
and filled my soul
with wonderment
and joy.

You are the reason
I was born;
to love
and know not anguish
for the absence
of the one sure measure
of completeness.

Grieco

Imzadi

You are my fortress and my peace,
the one I pin my hopes upon
and yearn to see
when morning comes.
In you I find my rest
when all around
is turmoil
and confusion.

You are my silent place
amidst the noise and bustle
of the world without.
And at the dawn
when sunshine
makes the world anew
you are my reason to begin
and rise to face the day ahead.

Through it all,
despite the trials and demands,
I carry you within
as bulwark 'gainst the cares
that worldly things impose.

And when the night comes,
sure and quick,
to mask day's damage done,
you are my shelter
and my calm
from which I draw my strength
to carry on.

Keep the Dance

In the darkness 'fore the dawn
when doubts assail
and regrets loudly speak,
you are there to banish all
until my certainty returns
and I am whole once more.

I am content to have it so,
to be renewed before the light
by touch,
by gentle reassurance
that all is right,
that all is as it should be,
and I marvel
that despite all else
it should be so.

Nowhere else would I wish to be.
No time else could claim me so
as here
and now
beside you
as sunrise comes
and creeping light
does steal upon the world
to rob me of my sleepful pose.

And when I rise
to face the still new day
I will find no greater treasure therein
than you,
my reason and my joy,
my present and my hope
for futures yet to be
safe
within the refuge of our love.

Grieco

You are my fortress and my peace.

Keep the Dance

A wondrous thing

To have been loved is a wondrous thing.
To know that there is one person
with whom all things are possible,
with whom no topic is off limits,
with whom the bond is such
that distance is no barrier to togetherness.

It does not come often,
this connection,
this link,
this bond,
perhaps once in every lifetime.
And when it does
there is no doubt
that this is the one thing
you can be sure of,
that fills the empty spaces
and makes all else right.

Peace and certainty,
happiness and comfort,
two souls touching,
blending as if one,
and having once known this
nothing will ever match it.

To have surrendered oneself
with no thought of gain or loss,
unreservedly,
with full abandonment of rhyme and reason,
to have yearned when there is no cause
save one,
to have had no purpose
but to exist in the fullness of joy,

Grieco

this,
this is love
which absence is most strongly felt
when we know it not.

And if it should not stay,
if we find ourselves again alone,
the knowledge that love was not a dream,
that it was and is still true,
that what once was can be again,
keeps us whole,
keeps us searching for the other half
though we may never again find it
in quite the same way
with quite the same fit.

And if by chance it does,
if we are surprised again
by the newness of it all,
if we find our inner self
mirrored in the heart of one
beyond all expectation,
beyond all reason,
beyond all doubt,
with all our faults and flaws forgot,
our blemishes erased,
and weakness turned to strength,
then our future is assured,
our past is made manifest,
and our today become complete.

Before I Knew

I loved you before I knew what love was.

Quietly, you stole into my heart.

It did not take long.
A gentle longing,
a lingering thought of happiness,
a chance
that tomorrow would be better than today,
that hope could be fulfilled
and not be the mere imaginings
of a soul too long without.

Our lives have different paths
without those secret moments
where the heart and mind are shared
and two become the union
of twin souls combined forever.

But it is enough
to know that you are there,
that hope lives
and a thousand tomorrows
are made possible by today,
this moment,
this love.

I loved you before I knew what love was.

Grieco

I Do Not Love You

You ask me if I love you.

I do not love you
in my heart of hearts
for love does not
reside in throbbing blood,
and pounding pulse,
though I feel it so.

I do not love you
in my mind of minds
for love is not a thought
though my every waking thought
is filled with you.

I do not love you
with these hands
though every touch
does bring sublime delight
in such a simple ecstasy of motion.

I do not love you
with these eyes
for you are more than vision
and float
as if a dream
upon the world.

I do not love you
with heart,
mind,
touch,
or sight,
alone

Keep the Dance

but every breath
of life reminds me
it is so.

I do not love you
but with every waking
moment of my life
and heart,
and mind,
and hands,
and eyes,
do not make it less,
or more.

And if I love not
the sun,
the breeze,
the very world I see,
I do not love you.

And if I love not
the rain,
the sea,
and every sunrise in the sky,
I do not love you.

And if I love not
peace,
and noisesome strife,
in equal measure,
I do not love you.

And if I love not
future hopes,
and present dreams,
I do not love you.

Grieco

The world,
my life,
my dreams,
my sight,
and as I love them not,
I do not love you.

Keep the Dance

The title of the picture struck me
and stayed within my mind awhile.
"Dance me to the end of Love."
as though the end of love
was something to be sought,
something worth seeking.

I, for one,
never want to find the end of Love.
I want to find the beginning
and the middle,
revel in its newness
and the fullness of
ripened, full-bodied love,
with passion and mellowed longing
hand-in-hand at the end of day.

Dance me not to the end
where music and the loving stops.
Keep me here where song still plays
and sweetness of the dance
keeps me longing for the rest.
Change the title
and let the rest remain,
keep the music,
keep the sweetness and the joy,
keep the Love,
keep the Dance.

Grieco

Be With Me Love

Be with me Love
through all my days
that hearts
should know their mate.

Let pain and anger,
lies and hate,
be someone else's fate.

Let me love
through all my days,
a simple fate but true,
and let me dream
through all my nights
a dream of loving you.

Keep the Dance

Let's married be

Sally, my Sally let's married be
and set our captured spirits free.
Sally, my Sally let's run away
and let this be our wedding day.

So kiss me once
and once more now
as promise of our wedding vows.
So come now my Sally
let's run now and fast
to start our future from our past.

Sally, my Sally why be so blue?
Can you not see my love is true?
Sally, my Sally why do you cry?
Have all your words of love been lies?

Then kiss me once,
then kiss me twice
to banish fear in me tonight.
Then come now my Sally,
come 'way now with me
and let us bride and husband be.

Sally, my Sally your father comes
and we must from his household run.
Sally, my Sally let's be away
before your father bids you stay.

So kiss me once,
then kiss me thrice
to speed us quickly through the night.
Come quickly my Sally,
let's mount now and flee

Grieco

and you my wedded wife will be.

Then quick to my horse
and quick through the trees
then plight our troth
'pon bended knees.

Oh Sally, my Sally let's married be
and set our captured spirits free.

Keep the Dance

Renewal

There comes a time
when you turn around
and know,
just know
that this is the one,
that this is the future
you had hoped for,
that contentment in life is possible,
that love could be more
than a lingering hope
fading like a dream
in the light of dawn's reality.

And in that instant,
that single defining moment of time,
all things become clear,
and possible,
in a way unthinkable before.

Nothing that has gone before matters.
All things are new again
and tomorrow
is a welcomed friend
once more.

Grieco

Wedding Advice

You are the foundation
of each other's lives.
It is on this,
that all else rests.

Be good to each other.
Expect no one else to be
if you are not.
Deal with the little things
that irritate you.
If you do not,
they will soon become big
and much harder to handle.

Be friends.
You will always
have someone to turn to
and even in disagreement
you will find common ground.

Listen.
It is not as important to speak
as it is to understand.

Talk.
But let your talk
be of what is important to you
so the other knows
what is in your heart and mind.

Share the simple things,
for it is these
that memories are built on.

Keep the Dance

Laugh and cry together
and be not ashamed
of joy or sorrow
for they will bind you
in common cause and life.

Love unreservedly.
Give all you are
and all you will ever be
knowing
that it is now that matters
and no one
can guarantee tomorrow.

Fear not for loss of self
but know
that in the union of two souls
there is that
which transcends you both.

Be happy,
and embrace this day
and all that follow
in hope
and the certain knowledge
that you will always be as one,
that together you are stronger
than you are apart,
that the world holds no challenge
that together you cannot face.

You are the foundation
of each other's lives.
It is on this,
that all else rests.

Grieco

Always

I find you in the essence of my life.

With every step,
I find myself beside you in my thoughts.

With every breath,
I find the echo of your fragrance
and I smile.

I lie beside you in the brightening dawn
and gaze at beauty slumb'ring there.

With every glance,
I wonder
at the chance of dream
wherein I lay awake.

I know not if I sleep
with you the dream
or if I wake
and you the dreamer be.

If I sleep,
then let the dream proceed
and love unfold its tender arms.

If I be dream,
then wake within this dream
else I vanish
as sleepy 'membrance of the night.

Always
will I stay within this moment,
to see you as I see you now

Keep the Dance

**forever as my life and joy,
and I will love you,
always.**

Grieco

A Woman's Plea

Whither thou goest
there too shall I be.
No matter the journey
I'll travel with thee.
No matter the reason,
no matter the call,
I'll be there beside you
in Winter or Fall.

Whither thou goest
there also shall I.
To rest not alone
but with you I'll abide.
And in midst of plenty
through Summer and Spring,
I'll share with you all
that the seasons may bring.

Stay with me.
Stay with me.
Stay with me here.
We'll never know sorrow.
We'll never know tears.
I'll bear you fine children.
I'll make house a home
and from me my darling
you never will roam.

Whither thou goest,
Oh let me be there
to watch o'er your footsteps
to see how you fare.
I'll catch you while falling.
I'll watch while you sleep

Keep the Dance

and all of your secrets
as treasure I'll keep.

Whither thou goest,
Oh please let me come
for I love you greater,
far greater than some.
It shall not be easy
to travel the way
but I would thus travel
than by myself stay.

I've packed all I'll need
to be there by your side.
I've hitched up the wagon.
It's ready to ride.
There can be no reason.
I'm ready to come
where you will be going
to sound of the drum.

Whither thou goest
I'll ask thee no more
to be with you always
upon foreign shores.
This one final time
shall I ask this of thee
for there in your face
do the answer I see.

Whither thou goest
then go there alone
if you will not have me
you must then atone
for your grievous folly
so laden with woe
then go from me quickly

Grieco

so quickly now go.

And if I should stand here
and tell you to go,
there is only one thing
I wish you to know.
You make up my future,
my present, my past.
My love for you darling
forever will last.

Whither thou goest
I'll here then remain
to mind all the seasons
of sunshine and rain.
And though you desert me
and I must here stay,
I'll think of you kindly
and each day I'll pray.

Whither thou goest
return home to me
wherever the journey,
wherever you be.
Wherever fate takes you
so far from my side,
I'll wait for you always,
I here will abide.

Come now my darling
and plough now this field.
We'll see then in Autumn
what bounty it yields.
Then in the bright sunshine
of some distant morn,
you'll be here beside me
when child is born.

Keep the Dance

Whither thou goest,
Nay prithee don't say.
Still linger, please tarry
for just one more day.
And if there is reason
why you should stay not,
my kisses are reason
for reason forgot.

Whither thou goest,
it shan't be this day.
Come lay down beside me.
Come with me now lay.
Come here and rest easy.
My blouson unlace.
Here lies your hearts future
in my warm embrace.

Then come to me,
come to me,
come to me now,
with fire down below
and sweat on your brow.
We'll harvest the meadow.
We'll mow down the hay
and here in my arms
you always will stay.

Grieco

Memory of your kiss

A kiss.

A touch.

Your scent on your pillow.

A lingering warmth upon the sheets
is all that will remain
in the faded light of morning,
is all that will remain
to remind me of you
during the empty time
while you are gone.

The warmth will vanish.
Your scent will disappear
but I pray that my memory of you
will not lessen as the days progress,
will remain strong
as the months pass by,
will be vibrant and sure
when you at last return to me.

And if you do not,
if misfortune takes you from this world
and me
then these memories must suffice
until I meet you hence
beyond this life.

Hold me once before you go.
Let me add this moment
to the treasure
I hoard against the time ahead.

Keep the Dance

Hold me so I might remember.

Kiss me and say goodbye.

Leave while I am still brave,
while I can still smile
and let you go.

Wave one last time
as you move from view
and I am left alone
with my hope,
my dread,
and my fears.

I can still taste you on my lips
but that too will fade,
but not,
please not,
the memory
of your kiss.

Grieco

A rose to remember you by

It is all I ever dream of
this sun kissed rose
and you
standing there
beneath the arbor
on the day before you left,
the day before you said goodbye
for the last time.

This rose remains here still,
here in the backyard,
but you are gone
to where I cannot go
except in dreams alone
where I can find you
and be whole again.

But I have this rose
to remember you by.
Curled upon itself,
as though asleep,
it waits for dawn's first light.

It is not bold.
It rests there silently,
expectantly,
for that dear touch,
a golden kiss,
to welcome it awake.

I do envy the sun
to kiss such rose,
while it,
in gentle bliss,

Keep the Dance

unfolds at touch
of its belovéd.

In my dreams
I greet you thus,
in soft remembrance
of love's first kiss,
unheeding of the day ahead
seeking only slumber
to return to you.

And thus be there
to welcome you awake
with sweet caress
and warm embrace
as sun does gaze
with fondness on the scene.

But dream withdraws before me
with casual retreat
and I must greet the day
alone
except,
except,
for a rose
to remember you by.

Grieco

At First Sight Too

My heart is not my own.
I lost it when I first saw you.

When I held you in my arms
I knew that nothing would ever be the same,
that you would be the focus of my life
from then until forever
and that nothing I would ever do
would be as important as loving you
and giving all I am
and all I will ever be
to see you safe,
to see you happy,
to see you as I saw you then,
regardless of the time,
regardless of the circumstance,
regardless of the pain
and joy that future brings.

For you are my Life,
you are my Happiness,
you are my Love,
and on this all else rests.

All else fades away as unimportant.
All else becomes but backdrop
to this central fact,
that my heart is yours
and has been
since the moment
I first saw you.

Keep the Dance

Oblivious

She adored him.
You could see it in her face,
especially her eyes,
the way she looked at him
as she held his hand
between the comfy chairs
they were both ensconced in.
He basked in it,
soaking up the private time
in this very public place.

No one seemed to notice
though it was clear
to any who might glance their way
that there was a bond of trust,
of faith,
of love,
that went both ways
though his was more measured
in its way
with age and experience
leavening his consideration
and his gaze.

And yet,
perhaps despite what lay unspoken
in the silence there between them,
hers was unconditional,
a measure of his place
within her world
and token of the depth
of their relationship.

Grieco

A lesser man
might have been jealous
sitting there unnoticed,
seeing all of this.

A better man
might have turned away
and let them have their moment
unobserved.

But I,
I merely sat there
transfixed by sight
of two so joined,
so bound within the moment
that nothing else mattered,
not the place,
not the time,
not even the other folk
chatting in the usual way
with nothing really much to say
sitting scattered there
around the room
oblivious
to a daughter's love
and a father's in return.

Keep the Dance

His Safe Return

Her empty tears of joy
fled down her cheeks
in search of happiness.
He was here
and she was safe
within his arms
where she had always thought
she should be
with contentment and joy
a sure result of her refuge.

But though her tears ran freely,
her heart beat no faster.
Her skin did not burn
at this slightest touch
and she felt the urge
to flee embrace,
this trap,
this ending of her hopes
and dreams of something more,
something greater,
something unique
that only she could offer.

Not wife.
Not mother.
Not helpmate
to a great or lesser man.
Not nursemaid to an ego
shattered by a careless word.
Not supporter of a cause
with no ending but his.

She turned to run

Grieco

within her mind
but she was held fast
by his arms,
by his ambition,
by his need for her
to be what his dreams
said she should be
and his spoken love for her.

She was a prisoner
of her hopes
and of her fears
with his embrace
the bars that brought
the surety
of her bond.

And so her empty tears of joy
fled down her cheeks
at his return
and she was lost.

Keep the Dance

All the difference

I have often wondered,
if I had it to do over again,
would I do it all the same?

I suppose I would
for the most part
in matters great and small.

But there is one thing,
one single thing,
which impact
would shape me
more than any other.

I would love less wisely.

I would give my heart freely
and let the chips
fall where they may.

I would be less concerned
with rights and wrongs
and follow where my heart led
regardless of the cost.

I would see the consequences
of those other paths,
those choices not made,
and been unfettered
by convention,
by duty,
by placing the joy of others
before my own.

Grieco

I would make
different mistakes,
hopefully better ones,
and not play it safe
but wander on untrodden paths
and lay by swiftly flowing brooks
until my heart was content
with the time,
the place,
the company,
and itself.

I would be more me
and less them,
more free
and less chained
by responsibility,
more open to possibilities,
more willing to find
what lay all around,
more focused on the now
and less on what could be,
if only,
if only
I had the courage
to let my heart rule my mind
and the will to follow
where my heart would lead,
to give myself completely
without reservation
or thought for tomorrow
or the day after.

I would not worry
but would savor every moment,
every instant of existence
from the first sweet conscious thought

Keep the Dance

to the last soft fleeting memory
of days lived
and nights experienced
in rapturous fullness
and subtle incompleteness.

'Til, having had my fill,
I rested
and dreamt of common things
made extraordinary
by the doing of them.

I would not hesitate
or pause
as common sense prevailed
but plunge in deeply
'til the way back
was obscured by passion
and denied to conscious thought.

Doubts are a present burden,
regrets a bitter dream
for those whose conscience
was their guide.

When unbending duty leads
and hopes are chained to others' dreams
the heart is but an afterthought,
a reminder of a life unlived
and burdens borne
at the expense of oneself.

It is not the wrong path,
it cannot be,
for it contains rewards and joys
unknown to others.

Grieco

But it is the more troublesome,
the one of sacrifice
and denial,
of dreams postponed
and hopes forgotten,
of roads passed by
and causes unchampioned.

It is the safe and silent channel
between the shoals of discontent
and the unknown ocean there beyond.

It is not without risk
but the risk is to a self
so restrained and channeled
to a certain fate,
that potential is lost
before the lure
of a clear destination
bounded by the known.

It is the path most taken,
the life most lived,
the choice most made,
rational and measured,
secure and safe,
with much of worth,
of meaning,
of value
encountered on the way.

And yet,
and yet,
I suppose,
that if I had it all
to do over again,
I would change one thing.

Keep the Dance

I would love less wisely.

**And that,
would make all the difference.**

Grieco

Regardless

Should the world end
and I alone remain
to see the aftermath,
I would miss you
most of all.

For regardless
of the rest all lost
you are the one thing
that would not,
could not be replaced
and I would grieve that loss
more deeply than all the rest
then vanished in an instant,
gone before the eye could blink,
removed by nature or by man
in simple savagery.

But if you should survive
then I would not mind
the end of all that is.
For I would count me blessed
to face the barren slate
on which a future could be writ
with all tomorrows possible
with you beside me.

And should the end be slow
then would I treasure all
that passed between the then and now
with every dawn a gift,
every day a surprise,
every night a mystery
that deep within its depths

Keep the Dance

the promise of the next should lie.

And when it came
with promise thus fulfilled
then would I embrace
the future thus revealed
and hope for more.

Hope that end could be deferred
but one day more
and then another still
'til all the days were used
and time should loose its grip
upon these wayward souls
that dared to love
and stay beyond the end of days
until they could not linger more.

Grieco

What is known

"I love you",
said the blind man
to his deaf wife.

"I love you too",
she signed in return
their hands
softly touching as she spoke.

It was clear to all present.
There was no need to explain
that what the eyes could not see,
what the ears could not hear,
their hearts knew,
their hearts knew.

Keep the Dance

With a kiss

With a kiss
I send you to your rest
and pray that angels
guide you gently
through the night ahead.

No stone can touch you now.
No name can call you forth
with anger at the calling.
No pain will assail you
nor will memory fail
as body falters
and betrays the spirit
nestled there
within unwieldy frame.

Sleep.
And in your sleep
know no more of mortal things,
of sorrow's
longing for departed friend,
of regrets
borne on the wind of necessity,
of chances
lost in the taking,
and knowledge
gained in loss.

Be at peace.
For cares have left you
with none to take their place
and furrows etched by time
have eased their grip
upon this most belovéd face.

Grieco

Dream,
if dreams are left you in your state,
no more to wonder at the truth of things
but to see with undimmed vision
and clear-eyed certitude
those things glimpsed
but darkly ere now.

What wonders does your spirit find
as unbound
it moves between the here and now
to what may yet be?

Leave us to our own device
for you must go
where your dreams do take you
while we must stay
and watch you go.
Mourn us not,
but think kindly of us
as you know us now.

Rest.
Gather strength for journey just begun.
I will tend what you have left behind.
You have no use for it now.

Be free.
And in freedom
travel now beyond those limits
frame entwined had brought you to
though it be far from here and me.

Let me brush your hair and set it so
with gentle care.
And closing eyes with grief filled touch

Keep the Dance

**I will send thee forth
with a kiss.**

Grieco

On the end of things

She had nothing left to live for
so she died.
Oh, not all together
and not all at once
but in each silent moment
in that empty house
that once held so much life.

Time crawled before her measured gaze
punctuated by the mantle clock
ticking out the cadence
of the passing day.

As the night approached,
she lit a candle on the sideboard
there beneath the mirror,
and watched as dusk
deepened into night
and night softly vanished
in the light of dawn.

She waited,
sitting there
day-in,
day-out.
She did not sleep
as candle after candle
slowly became but spattered wax
within the simple pewter holder
he had given her so long ago.

It was a gift he'd said
to mark the morning of their meeting
in November,

Keep the Dance

in the candle shop,
down by the bay.

It was cold,
with the frost
thick upon the windowpanes,
and a brisk, sharp wind
drove them both indoors
against their will
to seek warmth
before continuing on their way.

It was not love at first sight,
but it was enough
that after they had said hello
and laughed about the cold
and chance meetings such as this,
that they agreed,
as people do,
to meet again.

They did,
and conversation
led to careful reconnoiter
of the souls of each
'til,
assured that each had met its mate,
conversation deepened into love
and they married.

On that day,
within their hotel suite,
he'd given her
that simple pewter holder
as a token of his love
and a sign that chance encounters
were not chance at all

Grieco

but fate
offering a future to us
if we can but see
to follow where it leads.

She used that pewter holder well
as a centerpiece each anniversary
and to keep the night at bay
with candle burning bright
each time he was away,
or late coming home from work,
or out in the tumult of a storm
as thunder crashed
and lightning burst with jagged light
across a rain swept sky.

It came to be a talisman, that holder.
As long as candle burned,
held by its pewter frame,
he would be safe
and would return to her embrace
to tell her of his journey.

Each time he'd leave
she'd place the holder in its place
upon the sideboard there,
and take a stock of candles
from their place within the drawer.

Then, as the first
would burn its last,
she'd take the next
and put it there to burn
to keep him safe
until he'd open up the entry door
and to her waiting arms
return again.

Keep the Dance

She never told him.
He would have laughed
and chided her
that she should place
so much faith
in such a notion,
that a candle,
in this holder,
would keep him hale and sound
against imagined threats
while he was away
on his journeys.

But it worked.
She kept the candles lit,
and for sixty years
it brought him back
to her waiting arms.

But candles cannot stop
the march of time
and no amount of melted wax
could keep him from appointed hour.

He simply did not wake.
It was before his lunch,
and tired he had sat to nap
upon his favorite chair.
But when she sought to wake him,
for his sandwich and his drink,
he would not.

Through the days beyond
she moved as though entranced.
Her body moved,
her voice thanked them all for coming,
and her hands busied themselves

Grieco

with all the thousand things
that must be done.

But her mind was still,
a silent echo to the world without.
She did not think.
She could not,
For every thought was filled
with him and life and joy
now gone,
now off on yet a final journey
with her behind to tend the things unfinished.

When it was done
and all had made their peace
and spoken words of comfort
and of praise,
they left
and she was alone.

Straightening the house
she listened in the silence
to the sound of empty rooms
and the clock counting out time
as the day passed.

And when her body
had completed the remaining tasks
she took the candles from the drawer
and placing pewter holder
in its accustomed place
put match to wick
and watched as flame took hold
and light grew
to hold the dusk at bay.

Keep the Dance

She sat and waited
replacing candles,
one by one,
as they failed
and went out.

She did not eat.
She did not sleep,
but sat as candles burned
and waited for his return.

Time held no meaning
and neither clock,
nor night,
nor dawn
gave cause for movement.

Only as each candle burned its last
would she stir
and place the next to take its place.

So she watched as candles burned
and waited for her reason to return.
And as the final candle flickered
with the exhale of her slowly failing breath,
he did.

Grieco

If I should forget you

If I should forget you,
I would forget myself.
For you are all that I am
and all I shall ever be,
intertwined with every moment of my life,
each breath I take,
and all the smallish things
that bring meaning to existence.

Laugh with me
that we may banish sorrow.

Run with me
that we may flee what lies behind
and find the promise of tomorrow.

Rest with me
that we may explore
the way two hearts
become as one.

Be,
just be,
and the world is a brighter,
better place
filled with memories
of your smile,
your voice,
your touch.

You make up the fullness of my life.
And if I should forget you,
I would forget myself.

Grieco

Compulsion

ABOUT THE AUTHOR

Born and raised in a small rural town, the author left to pursue higher education and a career which took him to different parts of the world. After a lifetime listening to the whisper of the wind, the burble of a brook, and the sound of songbirds all imparting their wisdom, he's returned to his roots, spending his days as a country gentleman, taking the time now and then to put some words on paper.

Find more from Pat at pat-grieco.com

www.ingramcontent.com/pod-product-compliance
Lightning Source LLC
Chambersburg PA
CBHW032146040426
42449CB00005B/419